Success journal

A DAILY PRACTICE FOR **POSITIVITY, RESILIENCE,** AND **GROWTH**

JON GORDON

Bestselling Author of *The Energy Bus*

WILEY

Published by John Wiley & Sons, Inc., Hoboken, New Jersey.
Published simultaneously in Canada.

Library of Congress Cataloging-in-Publication Data is Available:

ISBN 9781119430414 (cloth)
ISBN 9781119430940 (ePub)
ISBN 9781119430827 (ePDF)

COVER DESIGN: PAUL MCCARTHY

SKY10076000_052924

Introduction: Why a Success Journal?

When my children were young, I read a story about United States gymnast Bart Connor, who was able to overcome a torn bicep muscle to win two gold medals at the 1984 Olympics. When asked how he did it, he explained that when he was growing up, each night before bedtime his parents would ask him his success of the day. He said, "Every night I went to bed a success. Every morning I woke up a success. When I got injured, I knew I was going to be a success because I was a success every day of my life."

I thought this was such a powerful concept, so I immediately began asking my two children about their success of the day. At first my seven-year-old daughter, Jade, didn't know what a success was, so she said, "I didn't beat my brother up today." I laughed and then taught her the definition of success. Eventually she and her brother, Cole, learned to share their successes with me and it became part of our bedtime ritual.

Since that time, I've encouraged people of all ages to think about and write down their success of the day. Instead of dwelling on all the things that went wrong that day, all the mistakes you made and all the people who frustrated you, think about and focus on the one great thing that happened, the one great conversation you had, the one event that made you smile or the one accomplishment you are proud of.

When you write down your success each night, you are programming your mind and brain to focus on success. What you look for you will find. What you focus on shows up more in your life. If you want to test this out, start looking for red cars on the road. You will start seeing more red cars. By thinking about your success of the day and writing it down in your success journal, you will create more success in your life.

You will go to bed each night feeling like a success. You will wake up feeling like a success. What you think about you become, so by thinking about success every night, you will become a success.

It worked for Bart Connor. It worked for my children. It worked for the tens of thousands of people I've encouraged in my keynotes over the years to write down their success of the day.

And my goal is that it will work for you.

It is why I created this success journal. I wanted to make it easy for you (and your kids, if you have them) to begin this practice and experience how it transforms your mindset and life.

My hope is that this journal will help you go to bed and wake up feeling like a success, and that as a result you will have greater confidence to overcome your challenges and create the life and success you want!

Your Success Journal

Here are some ideas to help you reflect and come up with your successes each day:

The best part of my day was . . .

Today I accomplished . . .

I feel great about . . .

I'm proud of myself for doing . . .

I overcame . . .

The one great conversation I had was . . .

Today I helped . . .

"Just because you may not see the harvest, don't let that stop you from planting the seeds. Keep making a difference. A harvest is coming."

DATE: ________

TODAY MY SUCCESS IS: ____________________

DATE: ___________

TODAY MY SUCCESS IS: ______________________

DATE: ________

TODAY MY SUCCESS IS: ____________________

DATE: ___________

TODAY MY SUCCESS IS: ______________________

DATE: ________

TODAY MY SUCCESS IS: ____________________

DATE: ________

TODAY MY SUCCESS IS: ________________

"Purpose is the ultimate fuel for our journey through life."

DATE: ___________

TODAY MY SUCCESS IS: ______________________

DATE: ________

TODAY MY SUCCESS IS: ____________________

DATE: ___________

TODAY MY SUCCESS IS: ______________________

DATE: ________

TODAY MY SUCCESS IS: ____________________

DATE: ________

TODAY MY SUCCESS IS: ________________

"Failure today leads to success tomorrow. The worst event in life is often a catalyst for the best."

DATE: ________

TODAY MY SUCCESS IS: ____________________

DATE: ________

TODAY MY SUCCESS IS: ____________________

DATE: ________

TODAY MY SUCCESS IS: ________________

DATE: ________

TODAY MY SUCCESS IS: ____________________

DATE: ________

TODAY MY SUCCESS IS: ______________

"Consistency is what creates excellence because we are what we repeatedly do, not what we say we'll do or want to do. We must be consistent with our attitude, efforts, leadership, teamwork, habits, and our pursuit of greatness. When we are consistent, we'll see that our outcome is determined by our commitment to the process along the way. It means that our actions are based on our commitments, rather than being controlled by emotion or events."

DATE: __________

TODAY MY SUCCESS IS: ____________________

DATE: ________

TODAY MY SUCCESS IS: ____________________

DATE: ________

TODAY MY SUCCESS IS: ________________

DATE: ________

TODAY MY SUCCESS IS: ____________________

DATE: ___________

TODAY MY SUCCESS IS: ______________________

"Life is hard, but you are strong. The struggle is real, but so is your ability to overcome it."

DATE: ___________

TODAY MY SUCCESS IS: ______________________

DATE: ________

TODAY MY SUCCESS IS: ____________________

DATE: ________

TODAY MY SUCCESS IS: ________________

DATE: ________

TODAY MY SUCCESS IS: ____________________

DATE: ________

TODAY MY SUCCESS IS: ____________________

DATE: ________

TODAY MY SUCCESS IS: ____________________

DATE: ________

TODAY MY SUCCESS IS: ____________________

"You have a greatness inside of you, and in every moment you have the capability to do great things. The best is yet to come, if you choose to believe it."

DATE: __________

TODAY MY SUCCESS IS: ____________________

DATE: ________

TODAY MY SUCCESS IS: ____________________

DATE: ________

TODAY MY SUCCESS IS: ____________________

DATE: ________

TODAY MY SUCCESS IS: ____________________

DATE: __________

TODAY MY SUCCESS IS: ____________________

"Realize that we don't create our world from the outside in. We create and transform it from the inside out."

DATE: ___________

TODAY MY SUCCESS IS: ______________________

DATE: ________

TODAY MY SUCCESS IS: ____________________

DATE: ________

TODAY MY SUCCESS IS: ________________

DATE: ________

TODAY MY SUCCESS IS: ____________________

DATE: _________

TODAY MY SUCCESS IS: ____________________

"Shift your perspective and realize it's not about *having* to do anything. You *get* to do things. You get to live this life."

DATE: ___________

TODAY MY SUCCESS IS: ______________________

DATE: ________

TODAY MY SUCCESS IS: ____________________

DATE: ________

TODAY MY SUCCESS IS: ____________________

DATE: ________

TODAY MY SUCCESS IS: ____________________

DATE: ________

TODAY MY SUCCESS IS: ____________________

"Someone could wish for something twelve hours a day, but if they aren't taking initiative to make it happen, then what good is all the wanting? We must measure desire in terms of actions, too."

DATE: ________

TODAY MY SUCCESS IS: ________________

DATE: ________

TODAY MY SUCCESS IS: ____________________

DATE: ________

TODAY MY SUCCESS IS: ____________________

DATE: ________

TODAY MY SUCCESS IS: ____________________

DATE: ___________

TODAY MY SUCCESS IS: ______________________

DATE: ________

TODAY MY SUCCESS IS: ____________________

DATE: ___________

TODAY MY SUCCESS IS: ______________________

"No matter what anyone says, just show up and do the work. If they praise you, show up and do the work. If no one even notices you, just show up and do the work. Just keep showing up, doing the work, and leading the way. Lead with passion. Fuel up with optimism. Have faith. Power up with love. Maintain hope. Be stubborn. Fight the good fight. Ignore the critics. Believe in the impossible. Show up. Do the work. You'll be glad you did. True grit leads to true success."

DATE: ________

TODAY MY SUCCESS IS: ________________

DATE: ________

TODAY MY SUCCESS IS: ____________________

DATE: ________

TODAY MY SUCCESS IS: ____________________

DATE: ________

TODAY MY SUCCESS IS: ____________________

DATE: ________

TODAY MY SUCCESS IS: ____________________

"When you face a setback, think of it as a defining moment that will lead to a future accomplishment."

DATE: ________

TODAY MY SUCCESS IS: ____________________

DATE: ________

TODAY MY SUCCESS IS: ____________________

DATE: __________

TODAY MY SUCCESS IS: ____________________

DATE: ________

TODAY MY SUCCESS IS: ____________________

DATE: ________

TODAY MY SUCCESS IS: ____________________

"When you encounter adversity, remember that the best don't just face adversity, they embrace it, knowing it's not a dead end but a detour to something greater and better."

DATE: ________

TODAY MY SUCCESS IS: ________________

DATE: ________

TODAY MY SUCCESS IS: ____________________

DATE: ________

TODAY MY SUCCESS IS: ________________

DATE: ________

TODAY MY SUCCESS IS: ____________________

DATE: ________

TODAY MY SUCCESS IS: ________________

DATE: ________

TODAY MY SUCCESS IS: ____________________

DATE: ________

TODAY MY SUCCESS IS: ________________

"Abundance flows into your life when gratitude flows out of your heart."

DATE: __________

TODAY MY SUCCESS IS: ____________________

DATE: ________

TODAY MY SUCCESS IS: ____________________

DATE: ____________

TODAY MY SUCCESS IS: ______________________

DATE: ________

TODAY MY SUCCESS IS: ____________________

DATE: ________

TODAY MY SUCCESS IS: ____________________

"Anything worthwhile takes time to build. We all want success now, but that's not how success works. After all, if we had immediate success, we wouldn't build the character we need to sustain true success. The struggle, adversity, triumphs, and victories are all part of the building process, and we must embrace all of it."

DATE: __________

TODAY MY SUCCESS IS: ____________________

DATE: __________

TODAY MY SUCCESS IS: ____________________

DATE: __________

TODAY MY SUCCESS IS: ____________________

DATE: ________

TODAY MY SUCCESS IS: ____________________

DATE: ________

TODAY MY SUCCESS IS: ________________

"Focus on the things that you have the power to change and let go of the things that are beyond your control. You'll be amazed that when you stop trying to control everything, it all somehow works out."

DATE: ________

TODAY MY SUCCESS IS: ____________________

DATE: ________

TODAY MY SUCCESS IS: ____________________

DATE: ________

TODAY MY SUCCESS IS: ____________________

DATE: ________

TODAY MY SUCCESS IS: ____________________

DATE: ________

TODAY MY SUCCESS IS: ____________________

"When you are humble you don't seek to gain power; you become a conduit of power for others."

DATE: __________

TODAY MY SUCCESS IS: ____________________

DATE: ________

TODAY MY SUCCESS IS: ________________

DATE: ________

TODAY MY SUCCESS IS: ________________

DATE: ________

TODAY MY SUCCESS IS: ____________________

DATE: __________

TODAY MY SUCCESS IS: ____________________

DATE: ________

TODAY MY SUCCESS IS: ____________________

DATE: ________

TODAY MY SUCCESS IS: ____________________

"Failure is not meant to define you; it's meant to refine you. Sometimes you have to lose a goal to find your destiny."

DATE: ________

TODAY MY SUCCESS IS: ____________________

DATE: ________

TODAY MY SUCCESS IS: ________________

DATE: ________

TODAY MY SUCCESS IS: ____________________

DATE: ________

TODAY MY SUCCESS IS: ____________________

DATE: __________

TODAY MY SUCCESS IS: ____________________

"You leave a legacy by living and working with a bigger purpose. You leave a legacy by making your life more than just about you. You leave a legacy by moving from success to significance."

DATE: ________

TODAY MY SUCCESS IS: ____________________

DATE: ________

TODAY MY SUCCESS IS: ____________________

DATE: ___________

TODAY MY SUCCESS IS: ______________________

DATE: ________

TODAY MY SUCCESS IS: ____________________

DATE: __________

TODAY MY SUCCESS IS: ____________________

“What you focus on in life determines whether you will experience peace in your heart. Today, focus on what you have, *not* on what you don’t.”

DATE: __________

TODAY MY SUCCESS IS: ____________________

DATE: ________

TODAY MY SUCCESS IS: ____________________

DATE: ________

TODAY MY SUCCESS IS: ____________________

DATE: ________

TODAY MY SUCCESS IS: ____________________

DATE: ________

TODAY MY SUCCESS IS: ________________

"There will be times
when you're tested, and
it will be convenient to
do the popular thing
or the expected thing.
But the right thing
may require you to go
against the crowd."

DATE: ________

TODAY MY SUCCESS IS: ____________________

DATE: ________

TODAY MY SUCCESS IS: ____________________

DATE: ________

TODAY MY SUCCESS IS: ____________

DATE: ________

TODAY MY SUCCESS IS: ____________________

DATE: __________

TODAY MY SUCCESS IS: ____________________

DATE: ________

TODAY MY SUCCESS IS: ____________________

DATE: ________

TODAY MY SUCCESS IS: ________________

"Great leaders don't succeed because they are great. They succeed because they bring out the greatness in others."

DATE: ________

TODAY MY SUCCESS IS: ________________

DATE: ________

TODAY MY SUCCESS IS: ____________________

DATE: ________

TODAY MY SUCCESS IS: ________________

DATE: ________

TODAY MY SUCCESS IS: ____________________

DATE: ________

TODAY MY SUCCESS IS: ____________________

"Every struggle, every challenge, every failure is meant to help show us who we are in this moment and how far we have to go to become all we are meant to be."

DATE: ____________

TODAY MY SUCCESS IS: ____________

DATE: ________

TODAY MY SUCCESS IS: ____________________

DATE: __________

TODAY MY SUCCESS IS: ____________________

DATE: ________

TODAY MY SUCCESS IS: ____________________

DATE: ________

TODAY MY SUCCESS IS: ____________________

"Our beliefs are demonstrated by what we say and do. We must make sure our beliefs align with our vision and goals. If we have big goals, we have to believe big."

DATE: ________

TODAY MY SUCCESS IS: ____________________

DATE: ________

TODAY MY SUCCESS IS: ____________________

DATE: __________

TODAY MY SUCCESS IS: ____________________

DATE: ________

TODAY MY SUCCESS IS: ____________________

DATE: ________

TODAY MY SUCCESS IS: ____________________

DATE: ________

TODAY MY SUCCESS IS: ____________________

DATE: ________

TODAY MY SUCCESS IS: ____________________

"Love creates trust, trust leads to commitment, and commitment leads to sacrifice."

DATE: ________

TODAY MY SUCCESS IS: ____________________

DATE: ________

TODAY MY SUCCESS IS: ____________________

DATE: __________

TODAY MY SUCCESS IS: ____________________

DATE: ________

TODAY MY SUCCESS IS: ____________________

DATE: ________

TODAY MY SUCCESS IS: ________________

"Don't be someone who looks back and says I should have done this or that. Live and work like you have nothing to lose and everything to gain."

DATE: ________

TODAY MY SUCCESS IS: ____________________

DATE: ________

TODAY MY SUCCESS IS: ____________________

DATE: ________

TODAY MY SUCCESS IS: ____________________

DATE: ____________

TODAY MY SUCCESS IS: ____________________________

DATE: ________

TODAY MY SUCCESS IS: ____________________

"To seize the moment, don't let your failure define you; let it fuel you. Don't run from fear; face it and embrace it. Don't let fear rob you of your love and joy for the game; let it push you into the moment and beyond yourself."

DATE: ________

TODAY MY SUCCESS IS: ____________________

DATE: ________

TODAY MY SUCCESS IS: ____________________

DATE: ________

TODAY MY SUCCESS IS: ________________

DATE: ________

TODAY MY SUCCESS IS: ____________________

DATE: ___________

TODAY MY SUCCESS IS: ______________________

"One person in pursuit of excellence raises the standards of everyone around them."

DATE: ________

TODAY MY SUCCESS IS: ____________________

DATE: ________

TODAY MY SUCCESS IS: ____________________

DATE: ________

TODAY MY SUCCESS IS: ____________________

DATE: ________

TODAY MY SUCCESS IS: ____________________

DATE: ________

TODAY MY SUCCESS IS: ____________________

"We all fail. It's what we do *after* we fail that determines what we build in the long run. Some of the most successful people throughout history have experienced great failures, but they turned their great failures into great successes."

DATE: ____________

TODAY MY SUCCESS IS: ______________________

DATE: ________

TODAY MY SUCCESS IS: ____________________

DATE: __________

TODAY MY SUCCESS IS: ____________________

DATE: ________

TODAY MY SUCCESS IS: ________________

DATE: ________

TODAY MY SUCCESS IS: ________________

"Behaviors drive habits.
And habits create
the future."

DATE: ________

TODAY MY SUCCESS IS: ____________________

DATE: ________

TODAY MY SUCCESS IS: ____________________

DATE: ___________

TODAY MY SUCCESS IS: ______________________

DATE: ________

TODAY MY SUCCESS IS: ____________________

DATE: ___________

TODAY MY SUCCESS IS: ______________________

"You will have moments when the last thing you want to do is to love, serve, and care. It is during these times that you need to remember your purpose. When you know your *why*, you will know the way and you'll find a way."

DATE: ________

TODAY MY SUCCESS IS: ________________

DATE: ________

TODAY MY SUCCESS IS: ____________________

DATE: ________

TODAY MY SUCCESS IS: ____________________

DATE: ________

TODAY MY SUCCESS IS: ________________

DATE: ________

TODAY MY SUCCESS IS: ____________________

Other Books by Jon Gordon

The Energy Bus

A man whose life and career are in shambles learns from a unique bus driver and set of passengers how to overcome adversity. Enjoy an enlightening ride of positive energy that is improving the way leaders lead, employees work, and teams function. **www.TheEnergyBus.com**

The Energy Bus Field Guide

Jon Gordon's international bestseller, *The Energy Bus,* has inspired thousands of businesses, organizations, sports teams, schools, and families alike, helping them cultivate positive energy, overcome adversity, and bring out the best in themselves and those around them. *The Energy Bus Field Guide* is a simple and powerful guide for putting *The Energy Bus* lessons to work. Using the 10 principles, you'll discover how to navigate the twists and turns that often sabotage individual and team success, and how to move in the right direction with vision, focus, purpose, and positive energy.

The Energy Bus for Schools

Based on *The Energy Bus*, the *Wall Street Journal* bestseller by lead author Jon Gordon, *The Energy Bus for Schools* teaches educators how to fuel their schools, themselves, and their students with positive energy. Research shows that culture and leadership greatly influence a school's learning environment and students' academic success. This book will help teachers work together to create a school culture where school leaders and students can grow into positive leaders, energizing their school culture as a united front.

The No Complaining Rule

Follow a vice president of human resources who must save herself and her company from ruin and discover proven principles and an actionable plan to win the battle against individual and organizational negativity.
www.NoComplainingRule.com

Training Camp

This inspirational story about a small guy with a big heart, and a special coach who guides him on a quest for excellence, reveals the 11 winning habits that separate the best individuals and teams from the rest.
www.TrainingCamp11.com

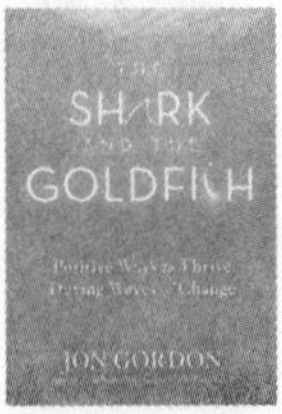

The Shark and the Goldfish

Delightfully illustrated, this quick read is packed with tips and strategies on how to respond to challenges beyond your control in order to thrive during waves of change.
www.SharkandGoldfish.com

Soup

The newly appointed CEO of a popular soup company is brought in to reinvigorate the brand and bring success back to a company that has fallen on hard times. Through her journey, discover the key ingredients to unite, engage, and inspire teams to create a culture of greatness.
www.Soup11.com

The Seed

Go on a quest for the meaning and passion behind work with Josh, an up-and-comer at his company who is disenchanted with his job. Through Josh's cross-country journey, you'll find surprising new sources of wisdom and inspiration in your own business and life.
www.Seed11.com

One Word

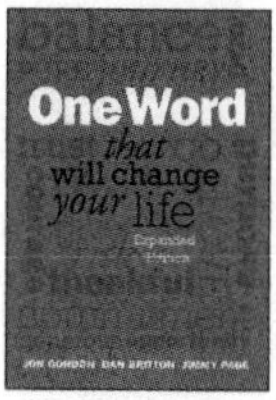

One Word is a simple concept that delivers powerful life change! This quick read will inspire you to simplify your life and work by focusing on just one word for this year. *One Word* creates clarity, power, passion, and life-change. When you find your word, live it, and share it; your life will become more rewarding and exciting than ever.
www.getoneword.com

The Positive Dog

We all have two dogs inside of us. One dog is positive, happy, optimistic, and hopeful. The other dog is negative, mad, pessimistic, and fearful. These two dogs often fight inside us, but guess who wins? The one you feed the most. *The Positive Dog* is an inspiring story that not only reveals the strategies and benefits of being positive, but also an essential truth: being positive doesn't just make you better; it makes everyone around you better.
www.feedthepositivedog.com

The Carpenter

The Carpenter is Jon Gordon's most inspiring book yet—filled with powerful lessons and success strategies. Michael wakes up in the hospital with a bandage on his head and fear in his heart after collapsing during a morning jog. When Michael finds out the man who saved his life is a carpenter, he visits him and quickly learns that he is more than just a carpenter; he is also a builder of lives, careers, people, and teams. In this journey, you will learn timeless principles to help you stand out, excel, and make an impact on people and the world.
www.carpenter11.com

The Hard Hat

A true story about Cornell lacrosse player George Boiardi, *The Hard Hat* is an unforgettable book about a selfless, loyal, joyful, hard-working, competitive, and compassionate leader and teammate, the impact he had on his team and program, and the lessons we can learn from him. This inspirational story will teach you how to build a great team and be the best teammate you can be.
www.hardhat21.com

You Win in the Locker Room First

Based on the extraordinary experiences of NFL Coach Mike Smith and leadership expert Jon Gordon, *You Win in the Locker Room First* offers a rare, behind-the-scenes look at one of the most pressure-packed leadership jobs on the planet, and what leaders can learn from these experiences in order to build their own winning teams.
www.winintheockerroom.com

Life Word

Life Word reveals a simple, powerful tool to help you identify the word that will inspire you to live your best life while leaving your greatest legacy. In the process, you'll discover your *why*, which will help show you how to live with a renewed sense of power, purpose, and passion.
www.getoneword.com/lifeword

The Power of Positive Leadership

The Power of Positive Leadership is your personal coach for becoming the leader your people deserve. Jon Gordon gathers insights from his bestselling fables to bring you the definitive guide to positive leadership. Difficult times call for leaders who are up to the challenge. Results are the by-product of your culture, teamwork, vision, talent, innovation, execution, and commitment. This book shows you how to bring it all together to become a powerfully positive leader.
www.powerofpositiveleadership.com

The Power of a Positive Team

In *The Power of a Positive Team*, Jon Gordon draws on his unique team-building experience, as well as conversations with some of the greatest teams in history, to provide an essential framework of proven practices to empower teams to work together more effectively and achieve superior results.
www.PowerOfAPositiveTeam.com

The Coffee Bean

From bestselling author Jon Gordon and rising star Damon West comes *The Coffee Bean*: an illustrated fable that teaches readers how to transform their environment, overcome challenges, and create positive change.
www.coffeebeanbook.com

Stay Positive

Fuel yourself and others with positive energy—inspirational quotes and encouraging messages to live by from bestselling author Jon Gordon. Keep this little book by your side, read from it each day, and feed your mind, body, and soul with the power of positivity.
www.StayPositiveBook.com

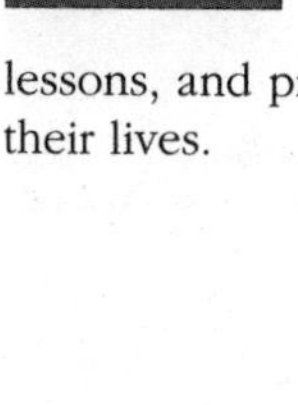

The Garden

The Garden is an enlightening and encouraging fable that helps readers overcome the 5 D's (doubt, distortion, discouragement, distractions, and division) in order to find more peace, focus, connection, and happiness. Jon tells a story of teenage twins who, through the help of a neighbor and his special garden, find ancient wisdom, life-changing lessons, and practical strategies to overcome the fear, anxiety, and stress in their lives.

www.readthegarden.com

Relationship Grit

Bestselling author Jon Gordon is back with another life-affirming book. This time, he teams up with Kathryn Gordon, his wife of 23 years, for a look at what it takes to build strong relationships. In *Relationship Grit*, the Gordons reveal what brought them together, what kept them together through difficult times, and what continues to sustain their love and passion for one another to this day.
www.relationshipgritbook.com

Stick Together

From bestselling author Jon Gordon and coauthor Kate Leavell, *Stick Together* delivers a crucial message about the power of belief, ownership, connection, love, inclusion, consistency, and hope. The authors guide individuals and teams on an inspiring journey to show them how to persevere through challenges, overcome obstacles, and create success together.
www.sticktogetherbook.com

Row the Boat

In *Row the Boat*, Minnesota Golden Gophers Head Coach P.J. Fleck and bestselling author Jon Gordon deliver an inspiring message about what you can achieve when you approach life with a never-give-up philosophy. The book shows you how to choose enthusiasm and optimism as your guiding lights instead of being defined by circumstances and events outside of your control.
www.rowtheboatbook.com

The Sale

In *The Sale*, bestselling author Jon Gordon and rising star Alex Demczak deliver an invaluable lesson about what matters most in life and work and how to achieve it. The book teaches four lessons about integrity in order to create lasting success.
www.thesalebook.com